Social Skills for Kids

Three Engaging Tales of Social Skills for Kids

Juan Carlos González

This book belongs to:

"The Fight of the Hens: Learning to resolve conflicts"

In Mr. Sam's farm, all the hens lived happily together in the coop. All except two: Mrs Rosie and Mrs Daisy.

These two hens couldn't be together without fighting. They pecked each other, pushed and pulled each other's feathers. This made the other hens feel uncomfortable and afraid to get close to them.

One day, Mr. Sam decided to intervene and talk to the two hens. He explained that their behavior was affecting the other hens and asked them to stop fighting.

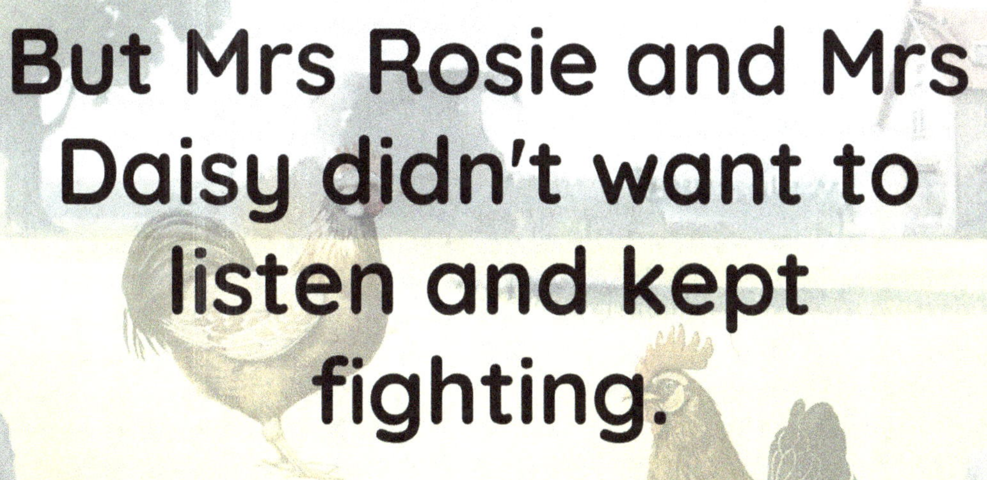

But Mrs Rosie and Mrs Daisy didn't want to listen and kept fighting.

Then, Mr. Sam decided to separate them into two different coops.

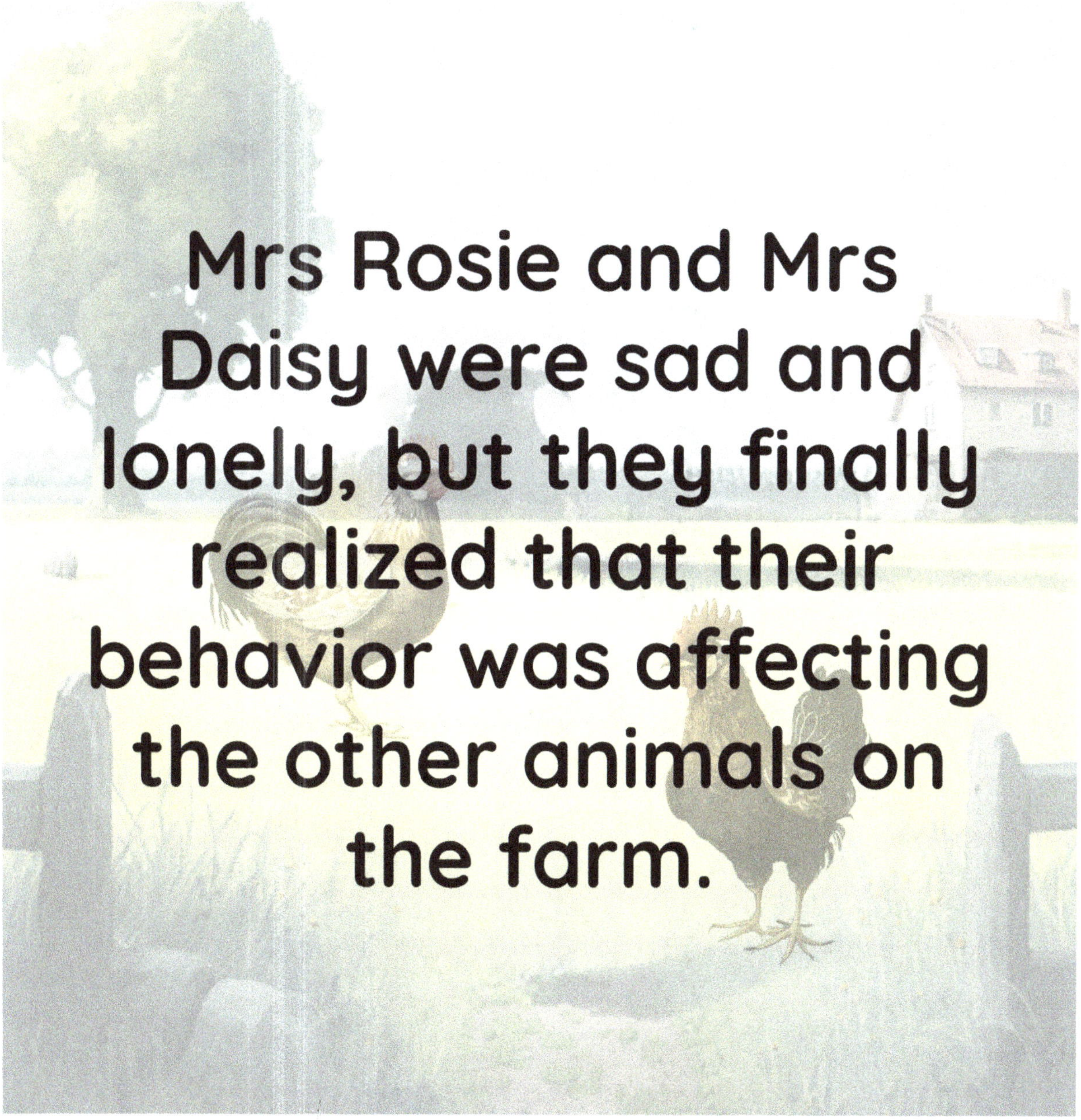

Mrs Rosie and Mrs Daisy were sad and lonely, but they finally realized that their behavior was affecting the other animals on the farm.

After a few days, Mr. Sam decided to give them another chance and put them together in a large coop.

At first, Mrs Rosie and
Mrs Daisy looked at
each other warily, but
then they realized that
if they kept fighting,
they would continue to
be alone.

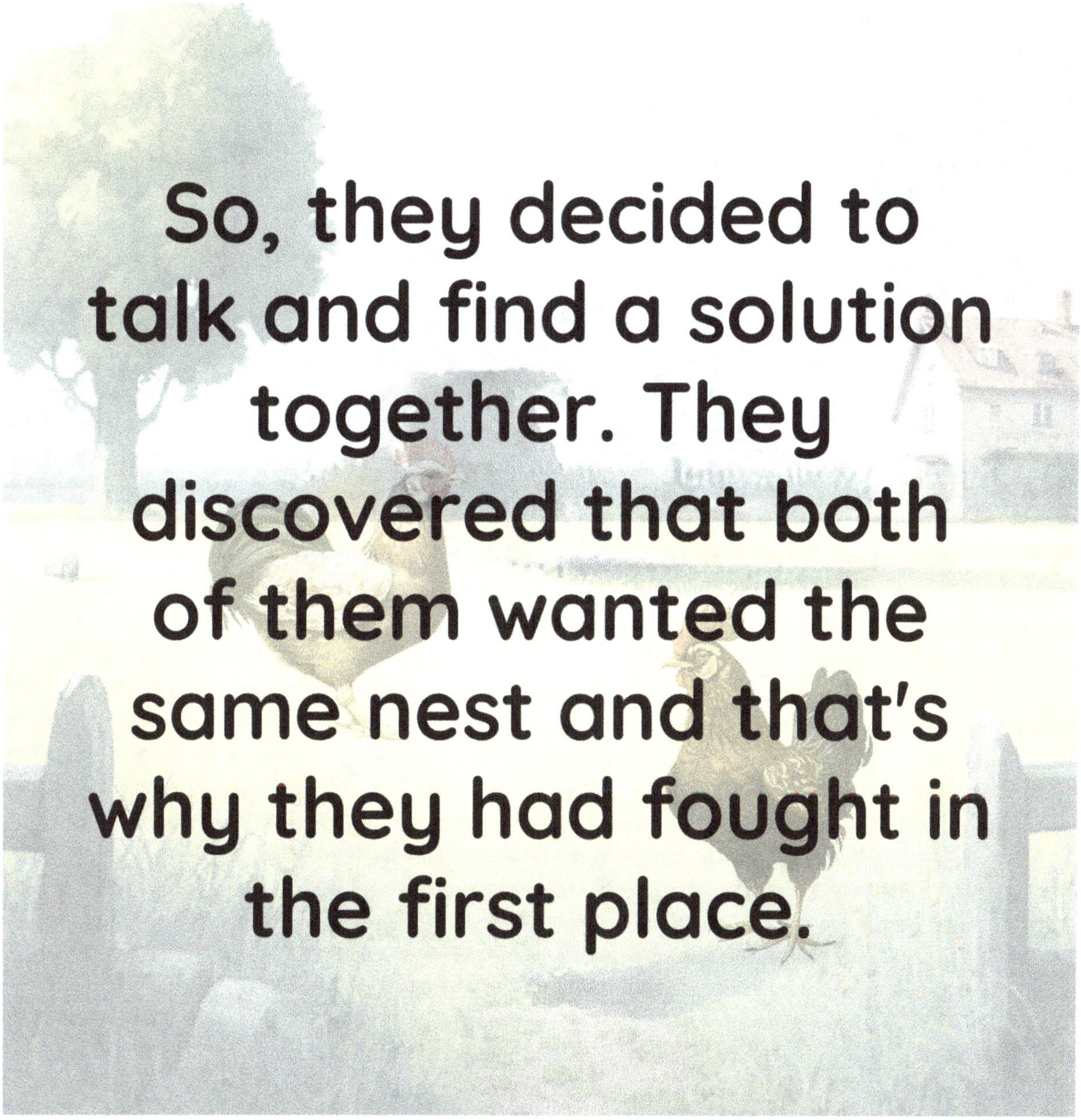

So, they decided to talk and find a solution together. They discovered that both of them wanted the same nest and that's why they had fought in the first place.

So, they agreed to take turns using the nest and committed to being friends and helping each other. The other hens observed the reconciliation and started to approach them. Little by little, peace returned to the coop and all the hens lived happily together.

Mrs Rosie and Mrs Daisy learned that working together was much more beneficial than fighting over things and that sometimes it's better to give a little to achieve harmony.

From that day on, the two hens became great friends and, together, helped the other hens on the farm live in peace and harmony.

"The Black Sheep and the White Sheep: Learning to Respect Differences"

In a lush green meadow, there lived two sheep: one was white as snow and the other was black as night.

Despite being very different, they were good friends and always had fun together. They played and frolicked through the meadow, but one day something changed.

While the two sheep were playing, a group of white sheep approached and made fun of the black sheep, saying she was ugly and different.

The black sheep felt very
sad and ashamed and
decided to walk away to
never see the other sheep
again.

The white sheep noticed
that her friend had
disappeared and searched
for her all over the
meadow.

Upon finding her, she asked her what had happened. The black sheep told her what had happened and the white sheep felt very sorry for her.

The white sheep realized that what the other sheep had done was wrong and decided to do something about it. She spoke to the other sheep and explained that it was not right to make fun of someone for being different. She reminded them that friendship and respect are important and that each sheep was special in their own way.

After listening to the white sheep, the other sheep felt ashamed and apologized to the black sheep. The black sheep felt very grateful and happy to see that her friend had stood up for her and that the other sheep had learned to respect her differences.

From that day on, the two sheep continued to play and frolic together, but now they had learned to value their differences and respect them. The other sheep also learned that we are all different and that makes us unique and special.

And so, in the lush green meadow, all the sheep lived in harmony and happiness, always remembering the lesson of the black sheep and the white sheep: learning to respect differences.

"The Friends' Corral: A Lesson in Teamwork"

Once upon a time, there was a corral where several animals lived: a pig, a horse, a rooster, and a cow. Each one had their own area in the corral, and they got along well, but they rarely worked together.

One day, a strong storm was approaching, and the animals had to make sure that the corral was well-protected.

But the pig didn't want to work with the other animals and instead stayed in its area, doing nothing.

The rooster, the horse,
and the cow worked
together to secure the
corral, but they couldn't
do it all alone.

That's when the rooster had a brilliant idea: by working together, they could finish the job faster.

With the help of the
rooster, the horse, and the
cow, the corral was
secured before the storm.

But when the pig arrived, it realized that it had missed out on the opportunity to be part of something important and helpful.

The pig learned a valuable lesson about teamwork and the importance of being a good friend. It promised never to let its differences drive it away from its friends and to work together for the good of all. And so, the friends' corral became an even more special place, where the animals worked together and enjoyed each other's company, learning to collaborate and appreciate the importance of teamwork.

To our bright stars,

Let these captivating tales inspire you to spread kindness, appreciate the beauty of our differences, and work together as a team. As you explore the pages of this book, may your hearts be filled with love, understanding, and the joy of creating lasting friendships.

With warmth and encouragement,

Juan Carlos